# Cool BREADS & BISCUITS

### Easy & Fun Comfort Food

ALEX KUSKOWSKI

**Checkerboard Library**

An Imprint of Abdo Publishing
www.abdopublishing.com

www.abdopublishing.com

Published by Abdo Publishing, a division of ABDO, PO Box 398166, Minneapolis, Minnesota 55439. Copyright © 2015 by Abdo Consulting Group, Inc. International copyrights reserved in all countries. No part of this book may be reproduced in any form without written permission from the publisher. Checkerboard Library™ is a trademark and logo of Abdo Publishing.

Printed in the United States of America, North Mankato, Minnesota
102014
012015

Editor: Liz Salzmann
Content Developer: Nancy Tuminelly
Cover and Interior Design and Production:
Colleen Dolphin, Mighty Media, Inc.
Food Production: Frankie Tuminelly
Photo Credits: Colleen Dolphin, Shutterstock

The following manufacturers/names appearing in this book are trademarks: Arm & Hammer®, Brer Rabbit®, Gold Medal®, KitchenAid®, Oster®, Proctor Silex®, Pyrex®, Quaker®, Roundy's®

Library of Congress Cataloging-in-Publication Data
Kuskowski, Alex., author.
  Cool breads & biscuits : easy & fun comfort food / Alex Kuskowski.
    pages cm. -- (Cool home cooking)
  Audience: Ages 7-14.
  Includes index.
  ISBN 978-1-62403-500-5
  1. Cooking (Bread)--Juvenile literature. 2. Biscuits--Juvenile literature. 3. Cooking--Juvenile literature. I. Title. II. Title: Cool breads and biscuits.
  TX769.K85 2015
  641.81'5--dc23

2014024344

## SAFETY FIRST!

Some recipes call for activities or ingredients that require caution. If you see these symbols, ask an adult for help.

### HOT STUFF!
This recipe requires the use of a stove or oven. Always use pot holders when handling hot objects.

### SUPER SHARP!
This recipe includes the use of a sharp utensil such as a knife or grater.

### NUT ALERT!
Some people can get very sick if they eat nuts. If you cook something with nuts, let people know!

# CONTENTS

# BITE INTO BREAD!

Offer your friends and family a special treat! Make bread and biscuits at home. Homemade bread is fresh, **delicious**, and it smells great too. Have a biscuit with breakfast. Make your own **sandwich** bread. Try a sweet **dessert** roll.

Cooking food at home is healthy and tasty. It can be a lot of fun too. Many canned or frozen foods include unhealthy ingredients. When you make the food, you know exactly what's in it. It's easy to make a dish that's **unique** to you. Cook a recipe just the way you like it. Add fresh ingredients to make flavors pop. You can even share what you make with others.

Put the flavor back in your food. Start making home-cooked meals! Learn how to serve up some delicious bread for your next meal. Check out the recipes in this book.

# THE BASICS

Get your cooking started off right with these basic tips!

## ASK PERMISSION

Before you cook, ask **permission** to use the kitchen, cooking tools, and ingredients. If you'd like to do something yourself, say so! Just remember to be safe. If you would like help, ask for it! Always get help when you are using a stove or oven.

## BE PREPARED

Be organized. Knowing where everything is makes cooking safer and more fun!

Read the directions all the way through before you start. Remember to follow the directions in order.

The most important ingredient of great cooking is preparation! Make sure you have all the ingredients you'll need.

Put each ingredient in a separate bowl before starting.

## BE SMART, BE SAFE

Never work at home alone in the kitchen.

Always have an adult nearby for hot jobs, like using the oven or the stove.

Have an adult around when using a sharp tool, such as a knife or grater. Always be careful when using them!

Remember to turn pot handles toward the back of the stove. That way you avoid accidentally knocking them over.

## BE NEAT, BE CLEAN

Start with clean hands, clean tools, and a clean work surface.

Tie back long hair so it stays out of the food.

Wear comfortable clothing and roll up long sleeves.

# COOL COOKING TERMS

HERE ARE SOME HELPFUL TERMS YOU NEED TO KNOW!

## CHOP

*Chop* means to cut into small pieces.

## BEAT

*Beat* means to mix well using a whisk or electric mixer.

## CREAM

*Cream* means to beat butter and sugar together until it's light and **fluffy**.

## BOIL

*Boil* means to heat liquid until it begins to bubble.

## CUBE / DICE

*Dice* and *cube* mean to cut something into small squares.

## DRAIN

*Drain* means to remove liquid using a strainer or **colander**.

## PEEL

*Peel* means to remove the skin, often with a peeler.

## GREASE

*Grease* means to coat something with butter, oil, or cooking spray.

## SLICE

*Slice* means to cut food into pieces of the same thickness.

## KNEAD

*Knead* means to press, fold, or stretch something such as bread dough.

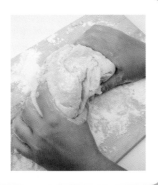

## WHISK

*Whisk* means to beat quickly by hand with a whisk or a fork.

# COOL TOOLS

HERE ARE SOME OF THE TOOLS YOU WILL NEED!

8 × 8-inch baking dish

aluminum foil

baking sheet

basting brush

bread pan

coffee cans

cutting board

measuring cups

measuring spoons

mixing bowls

peeler

rolling pin

rubber spatula

saucepan

spatula

whisk

wooden skewers

# COOL INGREDIENTS

HERE ARE SOME OF THE INGREDIENTS YOU WILL NEED!

active dry yeast

all-purpose flour

allspice

applesauce

baking soda

bread flour

brown sugar

butter

cornmeal

dried oregano

dried rosemary

eggs

garlic powder

ground cinnamon

ground nutmeg

instant yeast

Italian seasoning

molasses

mozzarella cheese

olive oil

Parmesan cheese

pecans

pepperoni sausage

premade pizza dough

rye flour

semolina flour

sweet potatoes

vanilla extract

white sugar

# MORNING MUFFIN BISCUITS

*Make a classically delicious breakfast bread!*

 **MAKES 6 BISCUITS**

## INGREDIENTS

1 cup whole milk

1 tablespoon sugar

1 tablespoon butter

1 package instant yeast

2 cups and 1 tablespoon bread flour

¾ teaspoon salt

1 tablespoon cornmeal

## TOOLS

measuring cups

mixing bowls

mixing spoons

measuring spoons

electric mixer

clean kitchen towel

dinner knife

frying pan

spatula

pot holders

**1** Put the milk in a bowl. Heat it in the microwave for 30 seconds. Stir in the sugar and butter. Let it cool.

**2** Put the yeast, 2 cups flour, and salt in a mixing bowl. Add the milk mixture. Beat with a mixer until smooth. Cover the bowl with a towel. Let it sit 12 hours.

**3** Stir the cornmeal and 1 tablespoon flour together in a bowl. Uncover the bowl of dough. Cut the dough into six equal pieces.

**4** Heat the frying pan on medium heat. Scoop out a piece of dough with a spoon. Be careful not to **deflate** the dough. Coat the dough with the cornmeal mixture. Place it in the pan.

**5** Cook the dough for 10 minutes. Flip it over. Cook it for 10 more minutes.

**6** Repeat steps 4 and 5 until all of the biscuits are cooked.

# BUTTERY HOUSE ROLLS

*Make your meals rock with this sweet roll!*

 MAKES 36 ROLLS

## INGREDIENTS

package active
  dry yeast

1 cup whole milk

3 tablespoons sugar

1½ teaspoons salt

¾ cup butter

1 large egg

3½ cups all-purpose
  flour

non-stick cooking spray

## TOOLS

measuring cups

measuring spoons

mixing bowls

whisk

wooden spoon

plastic wrap

baking sheet

rolling pin

round cookie cutter

clean kitchen towel

pot holders

1 Whisk the yeast and ¼ cup hot water together. Let it sit 5 minutes. Heat the milk in the microwave for 1 minute. Pour the milk into a large bowl. Stir in the sugar, salt, and ¼ cup butter. Whisk in the yeast mixture and egg.

2 Add the flour. Stir until the mixture becomes doughy. Sprinkle flour on a clean surface. Set the dough on the flour. Knead it for 4 or 5 minutes, until it is smooth. Put the dough in a bowl. Cover the bowl with plastic wrap. Let it sit 90 minutes.

3 Preheat the oven to 350 degrees. Grease the baking sheet with cooking spray. Melt ½ cup butter in the microwave.

4 Uncover the dough. Punch the dough down.

5 Roll out the dough until it's ½ inch (1.3 cm) thick.

6 Use the cookie cutter to cut circles of dough. Dip them in the melted butter. Fold them in half and place them on the baking sheet. Cover the baking sheet with a towel. Let it sit 30 minutes. Remove the towel. Bake for 30 minutes.

# CLASSIC SANDWICH BREAD

*Slice up this fresh bread and make a delicious sandwich!*

 MAKES 3 LOAVES

## INGREDIENTS

1½ tablespoons salt

1½ tablespoons active dry yeast

4½ cups all-purpose flour

2 cups semolina flour

non-stick cooking spray

## TOOLS

measuring cups

measuring spoons

mixing spoon

large mixing bowl

clean kitchen towel

plastic wrap

bread pan

sharp knife

pot holders

1  Put the salt, yeast, and 3 cups warm water in a mixing bowl. Stir. Let it sit 10 minutes.

2  Add the all-purpose flour and semolina flour. Stir until a sticky dough forms, about 5 minutes.

3  Cover the bowl with a towel. Let it sit 2 hours. Punch the dough down lightly. Cover the bowl with plastic wrap. Chill the dough in the refrigerator overnight.

4  Preheat the oven to 450 degrees. Grease the bread pan with cooking spray. Cover your hands with flour. Form one-third of the dough into a loaf shape.

5  Place the dough in the bread pan.

6  Make several shallow, **diagonal** cuts on the top of the loaf. Bake 35 minutes. Take it out of the oven and let it cool.

7  Repeat steps 4 through 6 to bake the remaining dough.

# SIMPLE ROSEMARY BREAD

*Watch these savory bread sticks disappear!*

 MAKES 1 LOAF

## INGREDIENTS

2½ teaspoons active dry yeast

1 teaspoon sugar

1 teaspoon garlic powder

2½ cups all-purpose flour

butter

2 tablespoons olive oil

1 teaspoon salt

1 teaspoon dried oregano

2 teaspoons dried rosemary

## TOOLS

measuring spoons

mixing bowls

measuring cups

mixing spoon

baking sheet

clean kitchen towel

basting brush

pot holders

1  Put the yeast, sugar, and 5 tablespoons of hot water in a small bowl. Let it sit for 10 minutes.

2  In a large bowl, stir together the yeast mixture, garlic powder, and flour. Add 9 tablespoons water, 1 tablespoon at a time, until the mixture becomes a sticky dough.

3  Sprinkle flour on a clean surface. Knead the dough on the flour for about 1 minute.

4  Grease a medium bowl and a baking sheet with butter. Place the dough in the bowl. Cover it with the towel. Let it sit 30 minutes.

5  Preheat the oven to 475 degrees. Knead the dough for 1 minute on a floured surface. Flatten the dough into a 9-inch by 5-inch (23 cm by 13 cm) rectangle. Place it on the baking sheet. Poke dents in the dough with the end of a mixing spoon.

6  Brush the dough with the olive oil. Sprinkle on salt, oregano, and rosemary. Bake 15 minutes. Take it out and let it cool.

# MOLASSES BREAD IN A CAN

*Make bread you can carry with you!*

 MAKES 2 LOAVES

## INGREDIENTS

butter
½ cup all-purpose flour
½ cup rye flour
½ cup cornmeal
1 teaspoon baking soda
½ teaspoon salt
½ teaspoon allspice
1 cup milk
1 teaspoon vanilla
   extract
½ cup molasses

## TOOLS

2 6 × 4-inch coffee cans
measuring cups
measuring spoons
mixing bowls
mixing spoons
whisk
aluminum foil
string
8 × 8-inch baking dish
saucepan
wooden skewer
pot holders

1. Preheat the oven to 325 degrees. Grease the inside of the coffee cans with butter.

2. Mix the flour, rye flour, cornmeal, baking soda, salt, and allspice in a large mixing bowl.

3. In a small bowl, mix together the milk and vanilla extract. Whisk the molasses into the milk mixture. Add the milk mixture to the flour mixture. Stir well.

4. Divide the **batter** evenly between the two cans. They should be about one-third full. Cover the tops of the cans with aluminum foil.

5. Tie string around the foil to hold it in place. Put the cans in the baking dish.

6. Boil 5 cups water in a saucepan. Pour the boiling water in the baking pan. Bake 2 hours. Stick a skewer through the foil into the bread. If the skewer comes out clean the bread is done.

7. Let the bread cool in the can.

# PEPPERONI PIZZA BREAD

*Try this mouthwatering cheese and herb meal!*

  MAKES 1 LOAF

## INGREDIENTS

non-stick cooking spray

1 egg

1 teaspoon garlic powder

1 tablespoon flour

premade pizza dough

6 ounces sliced pepperoni sausage

1½ cups shredded mozzarella cheese

¼ cup Parmesan cheese

1½ teaspoons Italian seasoning

## TOOLS

baking sheet

measuring spoons

mixing bowl

mixing spoon

cutting board

rolling pin

basting brush

measuring cups

pot holders

sharp knife

**1** Preheat the oven to 375 degrees. Grease a baking sheet with cooking spray. Mix the egg and the garlic powder together in a small bowl.

**2** Sprinkle the flour on the cutting board. Set the pizza dough on the cutting board. Roll the dough into a 12-inch by 9-inch (30 cm by 23 cm) rectangle. Brush the dough with the egg mixture.

**3** Arrange the pepperoni, mozzarella cheese, and Parmesan cheese on the dough. Sprinkle on the Italian seasoning.

**4** Starting at one long edge, roll up the dough. Pinch the ends closed.

**5** Put the dough on the baking sheet with the seam facing down. Bake 40 minutes. Take the roll out of the oven. Cut it into slices.

# STICKY CINNAMON ROLLS

*Get the cinnamon craze with a bite of these tasty treats!*

 MAKES 12 ROLLS

## INGREDIENTS

¾ cup milk
¾ cup butter
non-stick cooking spray
3 cups all-purpose flour
2¼ teaspoon instant yeast
1¼ cup brown sugar
½ teaspoon salt
1 egg
1¼ tablespoons ground cinnamon

## TOOLS

measuring cups
small bowl
8 × 8-inch baking dish
large mixing bowl
measuring spoons
rubber spatula
cutting board
clean kitchen towel
rolling pin
sharp knife
pot holders

1  Put the milk in a small bowl. Heat it in the microwave for 1 minute. Add ¼ cup butter. Stir until the butter is melted. Grease the baking dish with cooking spray.

2  In a large bowl, mix together 3 cups flour, yeast, ¼ cup brown sugar, and salt. Stir in the milk mixture, egg, and ¼ cup water.

3  Sprinkle flour on a cutting board. Set the dough on the flour. Knead it until it's smooth. Put the dough in a bowl. Cover the bowl with a towel. Let it sit 10 minutes.

4  Mix 1 cup brown sugar, cinnamon, and ½ cup butter in a small bowl.

5  Roll out the dough into a 12-inch by 5-inch (30 cm by 13 cm) rectangle. Spread the brown sugar mixture over the dough.

6  Roll up the dough starting at a short edge.

7  Slice the roll into 12 pieces. Place the slices on their sides in the baking dish. Cover the dish and let it sit 30 minutes. Preheat the oven to 375 degrees. Bake 25 to 30 minutes. Remove the dish from the oven. Let the rolls cool.

# SWEET POTATO BREAD

*Spread on some butter for a sweet taste!*

  MAKES 1 LOAF

## INGREDIENTS

1 sweet potato
non-stick cooking spray
¾ cup brown sugar
¾ cup white sugar
½ cup butter
2 eggs
⅓ cup applesauce
1¾ cups all-purpose flour
1 teaspoon baking soda
½ teaspoon salt
½ teaspoon ground cinnamon
½ teaspoon ground nutmeg
½ cup chopped pecans

## TOOLS

peeler
sharp knife
cutting board
measuring cups
saucepan
strainer
mixing bowls
fork
bread pan
electric mixer
whisk
measuring spoons
rubber spatula
pot holders

1 Peel the sweet potato. Cut it into ½-inch (1.3 cm) cubes. Boil 4 cups water in a saucepan. Add the sweet potato cubes. Cook 12 minutes. Drain the potatoes and place them in a mixing bowl. Mash the potatoes with a fork.

2 Preheat the oven to 350 degrees. Grease the bread pan with cooking spray.

3 In a small mixing bowl, cream the brown sugar, white sugar, and butter. Whisk in the eggs and applesauce.

4 In a large mixing bowl combine the flour, baking soda, salt, cinnamon, and nutmeg. Add the sugar mixture to the flour mixture. Stir well.

5 Stir in the mashed sweet potatoes and nuts.

6 Pour the **batter** into the bread pan. Bake 60 minutes. Remove the pan from the oven. Let it cool.

# CONCLUSION

This book has some seriously **delicious** bread recipes! But don't stop there. Get creative. Add your favorite ingredients to the recipes. Cook them your way.

Check out other types of home cooking. Make tasty main dishes, soups, **salads**, drinks, and even **desserts**. Put together a meal everyone will cheer for.

## WEBSITES

To learn more about Cool Home Cooking, visit booklinks.abdopublishing.com. These links are routinely monitored and updated to provide the most current information available.

# GLOSSARY

batter – a thin mixture of flour, water, and other ingredients used in baking and frying.

colander – a bowl with small holes in it used to drain food.

deflate – to release or squeeze air out of something.

delicious – very pleasing to taste or smell.

dessert – a sweet food, such as fruit, ice cream, or pastry, served after a meal.

diagonal – in a slanting direction.

fluffy – soft and light.

permission – when a person in charge says it's okay to do something.

salad – a mixture of raw vegetables usually served with a dressing.

sandwich – two pieces of bread with a filling, such as meat, cheese, or peanut butter, between them.

unique – different, unusual, or special.

# INDEX